IMAGINED CORNERS

Published 2004
by

STACK BOOKS

Smokestack Books
PO Box 408, Middlesbrough TS5 6WA
Tel : 01642 813997
e-mail : info@smokestack-books.co.uk
www.smokestack-books.co.uk

Copyright Keith Armstrong 2004
All rights reserved

Photo of author by Tony Whittle

Cover design and print by
Archetype Tel: 0870 2245 151
www.archetype-uk.com

ISBN 0-9548691-0-9

Smokestack Books
gratefully acknowledges the support of
Middlesbrough Borough Council
and Arts Council North East.

Smokestack Books is a member of
Independent Northern Publishers
www.northernpublishers.co.uk

For my mother, father and sister

IMAGINED CORNERS

Keith Armstrong

Acknowledgements

Some of these poems have been previously published in the following: *Pains Of Class* (Artery Publications, London 1982); *Dreaming North* (Portcullis Press, Gateshead Libraries 1986) ; *The Jinglin' Geordie: Selected Poems 1970-1990* (The Common Trust & Rookbook Publications, Edinburgh 1991) ; *Poets' Voices* (Durham County Council & Tubingen Cultural Office, Tubingen 1991) ; *The Hexham Riot* (Northern Voices & Crowquill Press, Belfast 1997) ; *Old Dog On The Isle Of Woman* (Cold Maverick Press Legend Series Number 1, Sunderland 1999) ; *Bless'd Millennium: The Life & Work Of Thomas Spence* (Northern Voices, Whitley Bay 2000) ; *The Town Of Old Hexham* (People's Publications, Seaham 2002).

The following poems carry specific dedications : 'Lady Jockey, Hexham Races' is for Miss Lamb on Rubislaw ; 'Saltburn in Bloom' is for Mark Beevers ; 'And Pigs Might Fly' is for Helmut Bugl ; 'Violins in Mittenwald' is for Anneliese ; 'Nightjars and their Allies' is for K.

Contents

My Father Worked on Ships 11
The Jingling Geordie.. 12
Voices Breaking 14
Folk Song for Thomas Spence..................................... 15
Tyne... 16
Peter Patterson's Ghost 17
An Oubliette for Kitty 18
To Kerry from the Isle of Woman............................... 20
Everybody's Got Love Bites but Me 21
Jogging to the Falklands 22
My Heroes... 23
Maud Watson, Florist.. 24
Turn it Upside Down... 25
Map of the World 26
And Pigs Might Fly... 27
Hermann Hesse in the Gutter...................................... 28
Just Like Our Mister Huber 29
The Statue of Hieronymus Bosch 30
Swan Song 31
Violins in Mittenwald 32
'All Rich People are Parasites' 33
Porec, Yugoslavia.. 34
Horses on Mount Vitosha 35
Senefelderstrasse 19, East Berlin................................ 36
Notes Towards a Poem on Russia............................... 38
Cuba, Crocodiles, Rain 41
The Divided Self 42
Melly 45
Saltburn in Bloom 46
Lady Jockey, Hexham Races 48
'Feare God in Hart'.. 49
Nightjars and Their Allies... 50
New Year, Newcastle 51

'At the round earth's imagined corners,
Blow your trumpets, Angels, and arise, arise...'
(John Donne)

'In Gateshead, we passed some little streets named after the poets, Chaucer and Spenser and Tennyson Streets; and I wondered if any poets were growing up in those streets. We could do with one from such streets; not one of our frigid complicated sniggering rhymers, but a lad with such a flame in his heart and mouth that at last he could set the Tyne on fire.' (J.B.Priestley, *English Journey*, 1934)

My Father Worked on Ships

My father worked on ships.
They spelked his hands,
dusted his eyes, his face, his lungs.
Those eyes that watered by the Tyne
stared out to sea
to see the world
in a tear of water, at the drop
of an old cloth cap.
For thirty weary winters
he grafted
through the snow and the wild winds
of loose change.
He was proud of those ships he built,
he was proud of the men he built with,
his dreams sailed with them:
the hull was his skull,
the cargo his brains.
His hopes rose and sunk
in the shipwrecked streets
of Wallsend
and I look at him now
this father of mine who worked on ships
and I feel proud
of his skeletal frame, this coastline
that moulded me
and my own sweet dreams.
He sits in his retiring chair,
dozing into the night.
There are storms in his head
and I wish him more love yet.
Sail with me,
breathe in me,
breathe that rough sea air old man,
and cough it up.
Rage, rage
against the dying
of this broken-backed town,
the spirit
of its broken-backed
ships.

The Jingling Geordie

Watch me go leaping in my youth
down Dog Leap Stairs,
down fire-scapes.
The Jingling Geordie
born in a brewery,
drinking the money
I dug out of the ground.

Cloth-cap in hand I go
marching in the jangling morning
to London gates.
Jingling Geordie
living in a hop-haze,
cadging from the Coppers
I went to the school with.

Older I get in my cage,
singling out a girl half my years
to hitch with.
Oh yes! I am the Jingling Geordie,
the one who pisses on himself,
wrenching out the telephone
his Father placed off the hook.

Listen to my canny old folk-songs;
they lilt and tilt into the dank alley,
into the howls of strays.
Oops! The Jingling Geordie
goes out on his town,
rocking and rolling a night away,
stacking it with the weary rest.

See my ghost in the discotheque,
in the dusty lights,
in the baccy rows.
Jingling Geordie,

dancing gambler,
betting he'll slip
back to the year when the Lads won the Cup.

Well I walk my kids to the Better Life,
reckoning up the rude words dripping
like gravy off me Granda's chin.
Whee! goes the Jingling Geordie:
figment of the gutter brain,
fool of the stumbling system,
emptying my veins into a rich men's-palace.

Voices Breaking

The bones
of young boys' voices
break,
splinter.
Panes of glass.
Pains of class.

Folk Song for Thomas Spence

Down by the old Quayside,
I heard a young man cry,
among the nets and ships he made his way.
As the keelboats buzzed along,
he sang a seagull's song;
he cried out for the Rights of you and me.

Oh lads, that man was Thomas Spence,
he gave up all his life, just to be free.
Up and down the cobbled Side,
struggling on through the Broad Chare,
he shouted out his wares
for you and me.

Oh Lads, you should have seen him gan,
he was a man the likes you rarely see.
With a pamphlet in his hand,
and a poem at his command,
he haunts the Quayside still,
and his words sing.

His folks they both were Scots,
sold socks and fishing nets,
through the fog on the Tyne they plied their trade.
In this theatre of life,
the crying and the strife,
they tried to be decent and strong.

Oh lads, that man was Thomas Spence,
he gave up all his life, just to be free.
Up and down the cobbled Side,
struggling on through the Broad Chare,
he shouted out his wares
for you and me.

Oh Lads, you should have seen him gan,
he was a man the likes you rarely see.
with a pamphlet in his hand,
and a poem at his command,
he haunts the Quayside still,
and his words sing.

Tyne

Rain is
fresh on my face.
My tongue is
wet with all the words
I've ever spoken.
Here Geordies like me have grown to speak.
They have travelled from hand to mouth.
Right from the first cry on Tyne,
the first trickle,
to this bitter river,
this flood of polluted words
that suicides drown in.

Peter Patterson's Ghost

Peter Patterson's ghost
haunts the Local History Section of our lives,
a lament threads the cobwebs of our shelves.
Imagine his hanging:
his head severed from his body,
his heart taken out and thrown into the fire,
his body divided into four,
his head and quarters
disposed of at 'His Majesty's Pleasure';
and the crying
of 'Innocent Blood',
the wailing of ghosts,
the terrible ugliness
of the Butcher's bayonet
raping
a beautiful day.
He is here to haunt this place forever:
This will be
'A Peter Patterson Heritage Centre',
an Annexe of Torture,
a brute of a Tourist Trail,
a journey through
Northumbria's entrails,
a procession of ghosts
through the deathly Archives:

the smell is a decaying Empire,
a Remembrance of Things Past.

An Oubliette for Kitty

There's a hole in this Newcastle welcome,
there's a beggar with a broken spine.
On Gallowgate, a heart is broken
and the ships have left the Tyne.

So what becomes of this History of Pain?
What is there left to hear?
The kids pour down the Pudding Chare lane
and drown a folksong in beer.

So here is an oubliette for you, Kitty,
somewhere to hide your face.
The blood is streaming from fresh wounds in our city
and old scars are all over the place.

There's this dirt from a history of darkness
and they've decked it in neon and glitz.
There are traders in penthouse apartments
on the Quayside where sailors once pissed.

So where are Hughie and Tommy, Kitty?,
the ghosts of Geordies past?
I don't want to drown you in pity
but I saw someone fall from the past.

So here is an oubliette for you, Kitty,
somewhere to hide your face.
The blood is streaming from fresh wounds in our city
and old scars are all over the place.

While they bomb the bridges of Belgrade,
they hand us a cluster of Culture
and tame Councillors flock in on a long cavalcade
to tug open the next civic sculpture.

And who can teach you a heritage?
Who can learn you a poem?
We're lost in a difficult, frightening, age
and no one can find what was home.

So here is an oubliette for you, Kitty,
somewhere to hide your face.
The blood is streaming from fresh wounds in our city
and old scars are all over the place.

So here is an oubliette for you, Kitty,
somewhere to hide your face.
The blood is streaming from fresh wounds in our city
and old scars are all over the place.

To Kerry from the Isle of Woman

This night
drunk in Newcastle's Arms,
not for the last time,
I can't see where I'm going.
In Kerry's bar-maid made-up eyes,
my restless life just lurches
between the stools and a City's bridges.
Noticing
someone like me or my father,
dressed to kill and die,
in local history pictures
on this pub's ailing walls,
I sup Tetley's Bitter along my life's blind alley,
looking for a goal to score
and someone to roar with.
I'm waiting for that stuffed Magpie in its cage
to let out a shriek with me;
Waiting for Godot
or brave Sir John
to buy me a pint,
a Season Ticket of Dreams;
and this Kerry waits for me behind the bar,
smiling a post-card from the Isle of Woman.
Slinking, a black cat, around the haunted room,
she lights me up my City's Walls.
Drenched hearts:
this night
drunk in Newcastle's Arms.

Everybody's Got Love Bites But Me

In this two-bit town,
it's once bitten twice shy,
chewing streets up and down,
my tongues asking why.

My teeth are on edge,
no work and no necking,
just sucking this ledge,
no future worth wrecking.

Nothing to say,
no reason to pray,
wish something lovely would hit me,
everybody's got love bites but me.

In the back of my mouth,
there's a taste of success
and word has it down South
you can talk oral sex.

But in this dingy town
my lips are all cracked,
speechless at home,
all sleepless and sacked.

Nothing to say,
no reason to pray,
wish something lovely would hit me,
everybody's got love bites but me.

Jogging to the Falklands

I get up in the morning with the Tele,
switch on at the same time every day.
I have my grapefruit and my little cup of coffee,
I keep fresh to earn my lovely pay.

I'm dynamic in the office with the typists,
with a telling and assertive voice.
I have no time for naughty unions,
I work hard to own my darling house.

Yes, I'm jogging to the Falklands
for my country,
jogging to the Falklands
to keep fit.
Jogging to the Falklands
with the family,
jogging like a mindless shit.

I have a very regulated schedule,
must accept the laws of life.
I've a lovely little daughter who's called 'Sarah',
a faithful and uncomplicated wife.

We have a little doggy we call 'Dennis',
and 'Margaret' cat's a spoilt but dear thing.
We pray to cleanse our sins each Sunday,
and then the joys of peace we sing.

Yes, I'm jogging to the Falklands
for my country,
jogging to the Falklands
to keep fit.
Jogging to the Falklands
with the family,
jogging like a mindless shit.

My Heroes

My heroes are fragile
not monuments of men.
They break down,
they are not pulled down.
They are special people but
no more special than you or I.
You won't see them
in the papers
or towering on hoardings.
They slouch rather than march,
they smile a lot;
and their collected works
are not collected
but grow,
scattered
in flower-beds,
between motorcades and
the stony silence of
war memorials.

Maud Watson, Florist

Bred in a market arch,
a struggle
in a city's armpit:

that flower
in your time-rough hand's
a beautiful girl in a slum alley.

All that kindness in your face,

and you're right:

the times are not what they were,
this England's not what it was:

flowers shrink in that crumbling vase,
dusk creeps in on a cart.

And Maud the sun is choking,

Maud this island's sinking,

and all that swollen sea is

the silent majority

waving.

Turn It Upside Down

Turn it upside down,
turn the coral into grass,
change a hard-hat for a desk,
stitch a flag into a dress,
turn it upside down.

Turn it upside down,
swing the land into the sea,
take an overall degree,
grow an acorn from a tree.
turn it upside down.

Turn it upside down,
take a flight below the water,
draw crosses in the slaughter,
shrink the floating voter,
turn it upside down.

Turn it upside down,
pull windows over curtains,
sew sparks into safety buttons,
ignite the United Nations,
turn it upside down.

Turn it upside down,
make a sea-bed of a reef,
walk a mermaid down the street,
squeeze sperm from a sheaf of wheat,
turn it upside down.

Turn it upside down,
Exchange the Stock for wine,
put the miner on Cloud Nine,
drown Britannia down the mine,
turn it upside down.

Turn it upside down.

Map of the World

We turned its global head as babies,
traced its edges onto paper,
scarcely scratched
the surface
of that old familiar spotted face
shaped up, boiling for a fight.

Hung on walls,
it looked so static
but in its latitudes and longitudes we knew
that people moved,
homes grew,
cities drowned,
and cliffs broke.

Later,
travelling,
we stepped out
across the sheet,
skipped
the Channel,
entered
new squares.
Then creeping back at dusk,
we folded up this map,
packed away the ice
and sunny beach,
stuck it all in a small back-pocket
and shrunk back
into our own world's frontiers.
That tiny territory
of our scars.

And Pigs Might Fly

On this evening flight,
necks stuck out,
we dart in formation
to a Stuttgart dream.
Complete strangers,
we share a common French wine
to celebrate clouds.
With your rough words,
you ask me what I do.
'Write poetry', I say,
and sign away a verse or two for you,
hovering in mid-air, between snow and sun.
'And you?' 'I breed pigs I do',
flying home from a swine seminar in Montreal.
To prove it, you sign me a photo of six of your litter,
the Swabian breed of Helmut Bugl.
It's a flying cultural exchange,
a rhyme for a slice of time.
The stars are sizzling in the thrilling sky
and, tonight, pigs might fly.
Tonight, pigs might fly.

Hermann Hesse in the Gutter

Headlong, headstrong
Hermann Hesse
fell, flat on his face, in the Tubingen mud.
'That's it! Get stuck into the shit!',
an ageing Swabian yelled.
And the church-bells throbbed along Lange Gasse,
and the dust fell on Heckenhauer's Bookshop.
And, as young Hermann slithered to his fumbling feet
and cleaned his shitty glasses,
his first poems
shone in the moonlit gutter.

Just Like Our Mister Huber

Just like our Mister Huber,
you've been drinking.
Just like our Mister Huber,
you drown the day.

Just like our Mister Huber,
you're swimming round the town.
Just like our Mister Huber,
with music on the brain.

Just like our Mister Huber,
a girl shines in your eyes.
Just like our Mister Huber,
you touch the evening sky.

Just like our Mister Huber,
you float between the trees.
Just like our Mister Huber,
you're dancing.

Just like our Mister Huber,
you're skating on thin ice.
Just like our Mister Huber
flickers in the candlelight.

Just like our Mister Huber,
you kick the Gartenstrasse leaves.
Just like our Mister Huber,
you kiss the soppy streets.

Just like our Mister Huber,
you lurch along the keys.
Just like our Mister Huber
blows his life away.

Just like our Mister Huber,
you taught us all to climb.
Just like our Mister Huber,
you fly, you fly.

The Statue of Hieronymus Bosch

Look down Hieronymus:
the blonde kids dancing at your feet;
barrel-organs churning songs out
against your deaf and cheesed-off ears.
Blink blind, stone-eyes,
cobble-cheeks,
dig the electric pleasure garden,
frame the nuclear canal
and sigh you weary statue you.

Chipped cloak,
cold painter's
nose drips with rain.
Drunk, we piss on the past,
slash and splash against the dark canvas.

Bosch, we still play the games.
I catch an angel bar-maid's eye
and swallow the blueness of it
in my aching head.
Beauty lodges overnight in the skull.

Unlucky Hieronymus:
missiles haloing your frown of a brow;
clouds crashing over the market-square.

They're building the greatest nightmare ever around you,
but your hands have grown too stiff to paint.

Swan Song

Oh you float on canals
on a head of Amstel beer.
You keep yourself white in a dirty town,
watching the tulips drown.
You skim past the red lights and the bulb-fields of traffic;
gracefully bend your vase-like neck
under a low Dutch joke.
The tall, slim houses seem to stoop
towards you;
you warn them off,
with a thrust of your beak.
You feed off tourists
on floodlit transparencies
broken by rippling houseboats.
You stay drifting in memories of the Indies;
a small piece of momentary beauty,
prettier than Amsterdam,
more shapely than Holland;
a true Swan
of the World.

Violins in Mittenwald

We can hear the craftsmen sounding
underneath the mountain streams.
They shape the bird calls round us,
they harmonize our dreams.

Each violin's a lifetime,
it is a blistering thing.
It's chiselled from the country's dying,
the years it took to sing.

Listen to the hammers knocking,
breaking up the day.
Each blow's a sparrow's heartbeat,
each path's a lover's way.

Sweet heart, the evening's falling,
there's a tune upon the breeze.
The craftsman's hair is snowing,
you can hear the cattle breathe.

Through the laughter and the killing,
the village band plays on.
This song was made for dancing
and a life was never long.

'All Rich People are Parasites'

'All rich people are parasites',
said the girl as she glided in,
drifting through the French window,
with a face that looked ready to kill.

She sat next to me on the chaise longue,
she had next to nothing on.
And Stockhausen's friend played piano
and the party became a song.

Her eyes moved amongst the guests,
cutting them up with her glare.
She draped her legs across mine
and played with the strands of her hair.

'All rich people are parasites.
The future belongs to the poor.'
And she put her hand on my thigh
and she kicked her shoes on the floor.

She took me upstairs to my room,
she was drunk on red wine and champagne.
In the rich afternoon we made love,
in the evening it spat on to rain.

Her hair was wild and soaked
as we wandered through the wood.
She fell and cut her leg
and I licked it to taste the blood.

In town we sat in a candlelit pub,
with the light flickering over our lives.
Somebody tried to sell us a rose
but she told him she wasn't in love.

'All rich people are parasites',
I'll forever remember those words,
and the evening we spent by the Neckar,
feeding the crumbs to the birds.

Porec, Yugoslavia

In this tender light,
the sun hangs:
a jelly-fish throb
stinging water.
Shoals of flickering moments
flash out of my sight,
with waves coax the coast,
nudging bony history
and wetting dust.

Porec
floats on the backs of fishes;
boaters sail through its streets.
Tanned tourists, knowing no better,
steal photographs of an old people crumbling.
Slides of a town
sliding into the sea,
such windows are sunken eyes;
sun-glasses
filled with rays dying.
The sun has fallen into the water
and we are drifting on clouds.
All aboard
the glass-bottomed boat,
watch us cast lines to catch
a glimpse
of some crushed tomorrows.

Horses on Mount Vitosha

They came through mist,
horses solid as trees
but warm and breathing,
with the wide world
in their broad brown eyes.
They were wise,
watched me sitting drinking wine alone,
then dipped their heads and drank
from a bubbling water-tap;
trotted off,
daintily avoiding stone-steps,
along the lane and out of sight,
threading through
the silent trees.
There was something in that moment.
A look, centuries-long, in their eyes.
You know, I think those horses knew
how life began.

Senefelderstrasse 19, East Berlin

In the oven of a Berlin heatwave,
this crumbling block bakes
and all the bullet-holed walls
flake.
Tenements skinned bare,
they burn with anxiety, death-wishes,
frustrated hopes.

From a cracked and peeling courtyard window,
a Beach Boys' track
clashes against an old woman's ears
as she carries a bagful of bruises home.
In this rundown, sunful flat,
I am tuned in to the BBC World Service –
a cricket season just beginning
and East Berlin sizzling
in a panful of history.

Senefelderstrasse 19, crawling with flies.
On top of the wardrobe, some volumes of Lenin slump,
there is dust everywhere, dust.
And all we are saying in all the sweltering
is 'Give me a piece of the Wall.'
just 'Give me a piece of the Wall.'

Look down onto the street –
the cobbles still stare,
the cracks in the pavement leer.
And, like every day, Frau Flugge traipses gamely along,
trying hard not to trip,
shabbily overdressed and hanging on
to the shrapnel of her past affections,
to the snapshots of her dreams.

From corner-bars,
the gossip
snatches from doorways at passers-by.
Inside, it is dark
and the money changes hands
slowly,

burning holes in the shabby pockets
of the dour Prenzlauer Berg folk:

'The People are strong.'
'They can't sit more than 4 to a table here.'
'THEY say it's illegal.'
'Let's sing!'

Amongst the clenched blossom of Ernst Thallman Park,
'a Workers' Paradise',
this glassy Planetarium gleams
under an ancient East German sky;
shining huge shell of a dome,
it traps stars and opens up Planets:
it is far-reaching, transcending walls.
It can stir the imaginings of all the World's children.
It is the light at the end of Senefelderstrasse.
It beckons,
beacons.

And me?
I am walking in blistered hours,
sick of the sight of money
and what it does
to all the people I love.
'A tip for your trip!
Instead of a brick from the Wall to take home,
bring back a Bertolt Brecht poem':

'And I always thought; the very simplest words
Must be enough. When I say what things are like
Everyone's heart must be torn to shreds
That you'll go down if you don't stand up for yourself
Surely you see that.'

Through the letterbox of Senefelderstrasse 19,
I push this poem.
And, for the last time, leave
through Checkpoint Charlie.
'Goodbye Frau Flugge, Herr Brecht,
the trams.
My friends, I wish you
sunny days.'

Notes Towards a Poem on Russia

i
Red star night.
A badge in the sky.
Banners at the cross-roads.
Oh Mother Russia,
you're past bleeding,
we are driving to the future
in a black limousine.

ii
Rubbing hearts
in the lift
with travellers,
an atlas in microcosm,
all telling us,
by their accents,
the rooms
that they were born in.
In the Ukraine Hotel,
the bathrooms drip
with voices
and many tongues
sleep,
with the last words of the day
melting away on their tips.

iii
Vodka is as warm
as a kiss.
It thrusts a burning finger
down your throat.
After a few,
we embrace.
Our arms surround
the World.

Warm Russian that he is,
Igor kisses me.
After fish and caviar,

the kiss
tastes good!

He signs away his writing:
'To Keith,
who is both happy and sad'.

Another night
spurts into a dream.
In and out of trouble,
people will always dance.

iv
TO A FELLOW WRITER IN RUSTAVI
Last night we swapped our shirts.
They didn't fit our bodies too well
but they fitted our mood exactly.

v
WHITE NIGHTS
The huge spread of Leningrad.
Cold courtyard heart.
The winter is hard,
but the nights are turning,
from black to white,
to red and back again.

vi
Circus,
and I'm dazzled;
not by the slender sway
of the supple trapezist
but by the spotlight
of a girl's blonde hair.
Shining from the audience,
she smiles
and all Russia smiles at me.
Such tricks in this moment.
I know I'll never see her again.

vii
ZAGORSK
All the wailing
behind fine railings.
The seminary domes like suns
catch the sun
and priests, with long nights in their beards,
harmonize brilliantly.
Their voices,
polished gold,
sound out the walls
as a rocket
glints in the sky.

viii
RUSTAVI STEEL WORKS
It's hellish hot in here.
Beneath the Earth,
these are
men and women
sweating steel,
forging
futures for
their children.
Steel bars for prisoners,
steel bars for playgrounds.
It's hellish hot in here.
Like a heart burning.

ix
Three swaying silhouettes.
Three bureaucrats.
Along the street,
they joggle towards us.
In their cases,
they carry documents with drink
seeping between the lines.

And now they are laughing,
and now the words are laughing.
They are peace documents.
Messages
meant for bottles,
meant for oceans.

Cuba, Crocodiles, Rain

It is raining on Crocodiles,
bullet-tears on the scales.
Here, where the balance of power has changed.
these banks of hardened green-backs, spread
stoned along the water's edge,
are caged
like old dictators,
reigns ended
as young Cuba
surrounds them.

The Divided Self

'Whene'er my muse does on me glance, I jingle at her.'
                                             Robert Burns

Such an eye in a human head,
from the toothless baby
to the toothless man,
the Edinburgh wynds
bleed whisky.
Through all the Daft Days,
we drink and gree
in the local howffs,
dancing down
Bread Street,
Like burns with Burns,
these gutters run;
where Fergusson once tripped,
his shaking glass
jumps
in our inky fingers,
delirium tugs
at our bardish tongues;
dead drunk,
we dribble down
a crafty double
for Burke & Hare,
heckle a Duncan Brodie
gibbering
on the end
of the hangman's rope.

In all these great and flitting streets
awash with cadies,
this poet's dust
clings
like distemper to our bones.
We're walking through
the dark and daylight,
the laughs
and torture

of lost ideals.
Where is the leader of the mob, Joe Smith,
that bow-legged cobbler
who snuffed it on these cobbles,
plunging
from his stagecoach pissed?
Where is the gold
of Jinglin' George Heriot?
Is it in the sunglow on the Forth?
We're looking for girls of amazing beauty
and whores of unutterable filth:
'And in the Abbotsford
like gabbing asses
they scale the heights
of Ben-Parnassus'.

Oh Hugh me lad
we've seen some changes.
In Milne's, your great brow scowls the louder;
your glass of bitterness
deep as a loch:
'Till a' the seas gang dry, my Dear
And the rocks melt wi' the sun'.

Oh Heart
of Midlothian,
it spits on
to rain
still hopes.
Still hope
in her light meadows
and in her volcanic smiles.
And we've sung with Hamish
in Sandy Bell's
and Nicky Tam's
and Diggers',
a long hard sup
along the cobbles
to the dregs
at The End Of The World:
'Whene'er my muse does on me glance,
I jingle at her'.

Bright as silver,
sharp as ice,
this Edinburgh of all places,
home
to a raving melancholia
among the ghosts
of Scotland's Bedlam:
'Auld Reekie's sons blythe faces',
shades of Fergusson in Canongate.

And the bleer-e'ed sun,
the reaming ale
our hearts to heal:
the Muse of Rose Street
seeping through us boozy-bards,
us snuff-snorters
in tobacco clouds.

Here,
on display
in this Edinburgh dream:
the polished monocle
of Sydney Goodsir Smith,
glittering by
his stained inhaler;
and the black velvet jacket
of RLS,
slumped by
a battered straw hat.

And someone
wolf-whistles
along Waterloo Place;
and lovers
kiss moonlight
on Arthur's Seat:
see Edinburgh rise.

Drink
from her eyes.

Melly

Something sad about clowns;
something thin between laughter and tears.
Pity the dignity, the love and the hate,
the twitching wire between body and soul
and you on that stage,
drunk on rum and borrowed blues again;
unique in the balance you keep to yourself -
never quite losing it,
never quite making it;
bawling out between Magritte and Morton,
playing the droopy-drawered clown
with yourself,
you

do the Melly-Belly,
the Ovaltine,
big brash belly-laugh blues.

Saltburn in Bloom

The Salt
is burning
the beaches.
Rocks are awash
with the embers
of seaweed.
We creep along Zetland Mews,
ships' cats in these cowering lanes,
searching
for wrecks in the daylight,
hungover
from last night's heartbreak
and Victorian times
still
ticking.
There is 'DANGER OF DEATH',
says a notice
in a jackdaw-scarred lane,
but in 'The (authentic) Victoria',
where the 'Whitby Cod' bakes
and the barmaid bends
to catch our looks
up her tiny skirt,
life leaps in our loins
and we lick the white
from our silky Guinness,
dreaming
of having her
in a Beach Hut or Teddy's Nook;
her scrummy Rugby League legs
waggling in the salt-air,
surfing
waves of wet
kisses.
We have a wonderful view from here:
with our eyelash tints,
it's a fine place
for smuggling memories
from the jewel streets

or snatching an antique moment
in the Cliff Lift.
And today we are drinking
like Smuggler Kings
in the 'Ship Inn',
singing old folk songs
in 'The Back Alex'.
Our lips crack
and the rain cries
down our faces:
we're dripping
like lost fish
adrift
in Saltburn Gill.
So spray
the Salt
on your local rag;
its Deaths Column
will burn,
like the fat
on that
barmaid's thighs!

Lady Jockey, Hexham Races

I am a lady jockey;
dark stallions
course my veins,
and my heart
pounds
with a herd
of wild-hoof beats,
blood pulsing
hot breath
of bold horses.
I jump the frantic fences
of my day-dreams,
eyes lit
with a glow of life:
I toss and turn
and thrash
in the sunlight;
my mighty steed
romps
across the warm grass,
heat
startling
my taut body.
I am joyous
to be alive,
skylarks fill
my thirsting throat.
I will ride
forever
breathing ecstatically;
an animal love
in my lungs;
and the smell
of a bold Northumberland
scenting
my bracing hair.

'Feare God in Hart'

The House Martins over this calm Green
catch the Sun on their swift wings.
They swim
through the warm breeze
in the gossiping 'Hearts Of All England'.
Today, their little souls pour with a local happiness:
they are making the most of a Global Village.
Filling in time,
flying in time,
they nest in my eyes,
skim
across the tears,
the bones of a broken wall:
'Feare God in Hart'
is carved in stone
above a dusty door
the Martins fly through,
ridiculing words,
weaving different strands,
their trembling tongues outstretched
as they flick across water,
alive on the wing,
delivering songs.
Their home is where the Heart is –
on the Roman Wall
or in South Africa.
My birds cross the deserts of a fading Empire
in spirited migrations:
I don't believe in God,
only House Martins,
frightened Hearts
and Walls
that will always crumble.

(Wall, Northumberland)

Nightjars and Their Allies

The nightjars and their allies
have their heads down in the woods today,
dreaming of wild nights,
a chance to sing on the flickering wing.
And you my dark-haired songstress
could writhe naked on a bed of their feathers
as I touch with my aching fingertips
the tips of your sprawling bliss
in all that lushness between the trembling trees.
For you are dusky,
silky-tailed and
white-winged;
you are my European Nightjar
churring as I make you
spring to life in shivers of moonlight.
White-throated and golden,
star-spotted and black-shouldered,
you straddle your strapping limbs around me,
wrap my leaping heart in charcoal ribbons,
fly me screaming in a flock of black birds
and drench me
with jars of night song.

New Year, Newcastle

i
New day.
Feet poised
above the clean snow.
Pen approaching the paper.
Some things I know.
The more I live
the more there is
to learn.
I am growing
younger
every day.

ii
Here again,
working out ways
of touching
without hurting.
Locked in a room
at the end of a corridor
at the end of the century.
The grey drizzle dampens
the shoulders of blackbirds;
damp leaves flicker
on the corpse of Parliament.

iii
This is a time
for love
if ever there was one.
A joy that will lift
the concrete
off our bones,
free the song from our throats,
release the words from libraries.

iv
We need
to see.
See ahead.
Eyes against the Bomb.
Eyes to learn
to read
beauty.

v
Another year.
A new number.
Cash flow problem again.
The River Tyne
is sick.
Gamblers stagger
(a little bit on the Side).
The same old drizzle
rests a film of fog
on stooped offices.
Where are they going?
Chickens flock in to roost,
lay eggs in board-room bowler hats.
Their nation once seemed real.
Now it is reeling.
English goose-pimples fade.
The church bells take
their traditional toll
and something is ending.
The micro-fish and chips
come wrapped in 'Crisis Specials':
"Only A War Can Save Us".
These are the bombs
in the post:
'A Requiem For A Loyal Commuter'.

vi
There is
a man
alone in a corner
moaning.
He is a gravestone.
He is everything
that is dying:
he is
the Managing Director;
he is
the Salvation Army Brass Band;
he is
Oxfam;
he is
the Bank (the Archbishop) of England;
he is
the War Cabinet;
he is
Uncle Tom Cobley, M.P.

vii
Look at him.
He is frightened of life.
He says prayers to Securicor.
He is bugged and alarmed.
Now, look at us.
Look at our children.
We have no guards on our bodies.
We are growing
younger together.
We are making a party of our lives.
We will dance on flags.

Notes

17 'Monday, Peter Patterson was executed at Morpeth, pursuant to his sentence at the last Assizes, for High Treason in obstructing the Deputy-lieutenants in the Execution of Militia Laws. He behaved with becoming Decency.' (*Newcastle Courant*, 10 October 1761) ; 'A disagreeable circumstance attended the execution of Patterson. The noose of the rope gave way, and he fell down before he was dead : the cart was then ordered back, and a new halter made use of; and after he had hung the time that the law required, his body was cut down and dismembered, according to his sentence. It is said that after he fell down, he exclaimed "Innocent blood is ill to shed!"' (*Sykes Local Records*, 1833)

28 The writer Hermann Hesse (1877-1962) was born in Calw. At the age of 19, he began working at Heckenhauer's bookshop in Tubingen. It was there that he published his first poems as 'Romantic Songs'.

29 This poem was inspired by a reading I gave in a Tubingen school, after which a teacher said that I was 'Just like our Mister Huber' - a music teacher who was once discovered slumped drunk over his piano in the music room. I later discovered that a Professor Kurt Huber was stripped of all his academic honours and executed for his part in the 'White Rose' anti-Nazi resistance network. The Nazis had previously allocated him additional money for his researches into German folk-songs. Sophie and Hans Scholl were also executed for their parts in the 'White Rose' resistance. Sophie Scholl went to the scaffold on crutches and was beheaded by an executioner dressed in top hat, white tie and tails. The Geschwister Scholl Schule in Tubingen is a comprehensive school dedicated to their memory.